Wiltsh

A DOG WALKER'S GUIDE

Nigel Vile

COUNTRYSIDE BOOKS
NEWBURY BERKSHIRE

Countryside Books
3 Catherine Road
Newbury
Berkshire
RG14 7NA

To view our complete range of books please visit us at
www.countrysidebooks.co.uk

First published 2016
© Text and Photographs 2016 Nigel Vile

A CIP record for this book is available from the British Library.

ISBN 978 1 84674 338 2

Photography by Nigel Vile

Produced by The Letterworks Ltd., Reading
Typeset by KT Designs, St Helens
Printed by Gomer Press, Llandysul, Ceredigion

Contents

Walk

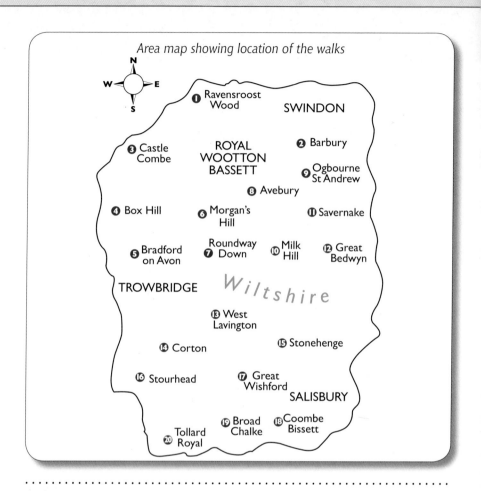

Area map showing location of the walks

- ❶ Ravensroost Wood
- SWINDON
- ❸ Castle Combe
- ROYAL WOOTTON BASSETT
- ❷ Barbury
- ❾ Ogbourne St Andrew
- ❽ Avebury
- ❹ Box Hill
- ❻ Morgan's Hill
- ⓫ Savernake
- ❺ Bradford on Avon
- Roundway ❼ Down
- ❿ Milk Hill
- ⓬ Great Bedwyn
- TROWBRIDGE
- *Wiltshire*
- ⓭ West Lavington
- ⓮ Corton
- ⓯ Stonehenge
- ⓰ Stourhead
- ⓱ Great Wishford
- SALISBURY
- ⓳ Broad Chalke
- ⓲ Coombe Bissett
- ⓴ Tollard Royal

PUBLISHER'S NOTE

We hope that you obtain considerable enjoyment from this book; great care has been taken in its preparation. Although at the time of publication all routes followed public rights of way or permitted paths, diversion orders can be made and permissions withdrawn.

We cannot, of course, be held responsible for such diversion orders and any inaccuracies in the text which result from these or any other changes to the routes nor any damage which might result from walkers trespassing on private property. We are anxious though that all details covering the walks are kept up to date and would therefore welcome information from readers which would be relevant to future editions.

The simple sketch maps that accompany the walks in this book are based on notes made by the author whilst checking out the routes on the ground. They are designed to show you how to reach the start and they contain a progression of numbers that relate to the paragraphs of the text.

However, for the benefit of a proper map, we do recommend that you purchase the relevant Ordnance Survey sheet covering your walk. The Ordnance Survey maps are widely available.

INTRODUCTION

Walking with Finn, the family Jack Russell, is always a pleasure, but also involves certain considerations. Roads and traffic are to be avoided if at all possible, as are fields with sheep and lambs, while even a slim and agile Jack Russell can find the occasional stile akin to an obstacle course, adding yet another factor to the equation. But, of course, there are many positives! Dogs love being in the great outdoors, and before a walk Finn gets so excited that he engages in what can only be described as vertical jumping!

I have always loved walking in the Wiltshire countryside, but for a dog it's the exciting scents and sounds that appeal. Water is always a great attraction, and not only for drinking. Finn enjoys nothing more than quite literally diving into a river or pond in the style of Tom Daley, often an amusing sideshow for passing walkers. A pub garden that welcomes dogs is also a must at journey's end, a place to rest and linger awhile after a pleasant few hours in the great outdoors.

This collection of walks in Wiltshire has been devised with all these factors in mind. Where there are sections of road walking, it is on very quiet country lanes where the chance of meeting vehicles is minimal. If there are stiles, they are those with enough headway and clearance for all but the largest or most immobile of dogs to pass through. In such cases, an alternative, or 'there-and-back' route has been suggested to ensure a decent walk.

You will discover waterside walks at Bradford on Avon and Great Bedwyn, wide open downland on Milk Hill and Roundway Hill, ancient history at the World Heritage sites of Stonehenge and Avebury, an Iron Age hillfort at Barbury, the southern Cotswolds by Castle Combe and the North Wessex Downs by Morgan's Hill. With all of this and so much more, this is a series of walks for every dog and its owner to enjoy. I wish you many hours of fun and relaxation walking with your dog by rivers, canals and ancient barrows in Wiltshire's beautiful countryside.

Nigel Vile

ADVICE FOR DOG WALKERS

Dog owners have some obvious responsibilities. To quote from The Countryside Code: 'The countryside is a great place to exercise dogs but it is every owner's duty to make sure their dog is not a danger or nuisance to farm animals, wildlife or other people.'

- Ground nesting birds can be found on Wiltshire's downland between March and July. Be wary of letting your dog run free in the area at this time. Equally, pheasants are often released in large numbers into woodland in the early autumn. Notices requesting that dogs be kept on a lead should always be respected.

- Sheep and lambs are by nature nervous creatures. As they turn and run, many dogs instinctively want to give chase. Such behaviour could cause a pregnant ewe to abort, so signs warning that dogs worrying sheep could be shot are not there for fun. Lambing time is between January and March. Always put your dog on a lead if you see livestock.

- A few dogs in Wiltshire have contracted the disease Alabama Rot. Although understandably very worrying for dog owners, remember only a very few dogs have caught this disease. The first symptoms are skin lesions on their legs, so be vigilant and if in any doubt, take your pet straight to a vet. Avoid muddy woodland and always wash your dog down after a muddy walk.

- Cattle are more often than not simply inquisitive rather than aggressive. A cow who considers her calf to be threatened in some way, however, is a different matter. The stories about walkers being injured by rampaging cows usually involve both calves and dogs. In such cases, the advice is to drop the lead and walk away, leaving the dog to sort itself out.

- There may well be horses along the way on some of these walks. It is best practice to put your dog on a lead if you see horses.

- Make sure your dog is never a nuisance to other people. With this in mind, it goes without saying that dog mess is dealt with properly, and that your dog is not allowed to jump up on other walkers enjoying a few hours in the countryside.

1

Ravensroost and Milbourne Common Wood

Following a woodland path through Ravensroost.

This walk a few miles west of Swindon takes some finding, being hidden away along a network of unclassified lanes. It starts off in Ravensroost Wood, ancient woodland that is a remnant of the former Forest of Braydon, a royal hunting ground in medieval times. Today this is

Dog factors

Distance: 3 miles.
Road walking: There is no road walking although a couple of minor roads have to be crossed along the way.
Livestock: None.
Stiles: None.
Nearest vets: Purton Vets, 77 High Street, Purton, Swindon SN5 4AB. ☎ 01793 771869

a nature reserve, with a rich array of flora and fauna. Oak and wych elm, coppiced hazel and the unusual wild service tree line the woodland paths, with bluebells and wood anemone, violets and primroses adding a seasonal splash of colour. To the south lies Milbourne Common Wood, part of a larger area of woodland known as Somerford Common. The UK Butterfly Monitoring Scheme have surveyed this site and found no fewer than 37 species of butterfly, an astonishing number considering the UK's indigenous population is just 59 species. Dogs always enjoy the sights, smells and sounds of woodland so this is a walk that will really go down well with your four-footed friend, especially with so many opportunities to run free.

Terrain
A flat and easy walk that follows well-defined woodland paths and tracks.

Where to park
The Ravensroost Wood Nature Reserve car park (GR: 024877). **Map:** OS Explorer 169 Cirencester & Swindon.

How to get there
Initially make for Minety on the B4040 Malmesbury to Cricklade road. At a crossroads in the village, take the turning to Brinkworth and Braydon. In ¼ mile, turn right to Brinkwork. In just under 2 miles, at a crossroads by a property, turn right along an unsigned road. In ½ mile, the car park is on the right.

Refreshments
The meadow adjoining Ravensroost Wood is an excellent spot for a picnic. In nearby Minety, the Vale of the White Horse Inn has a garden overlooking a large pond and allows dogs in the bar area. ☎ 01666 860175. **Postcode:** SN16 9QY

The Walk

1 From the parking area, follow the main path into the woodland for 600 yards to reach a gate and track. Along the way, the path passes a small pond on the left as well as a former shooting hut by a crossroads. Turn left along to a junction with a byway in 200 yards. Turn left and follow this byway for ¼ mile down to a quiet lane. Cross this lane and continue following the byway opposite for ¼ mile down to another quiet lane.

2 Cross over and follow the byway opposite that enters **Milbourne Common Wood**. This byway is shown on the OS Explorer map as **Blackberry Lane**.

Pippin is ready and waiting to explore the Wiltshire countryside.

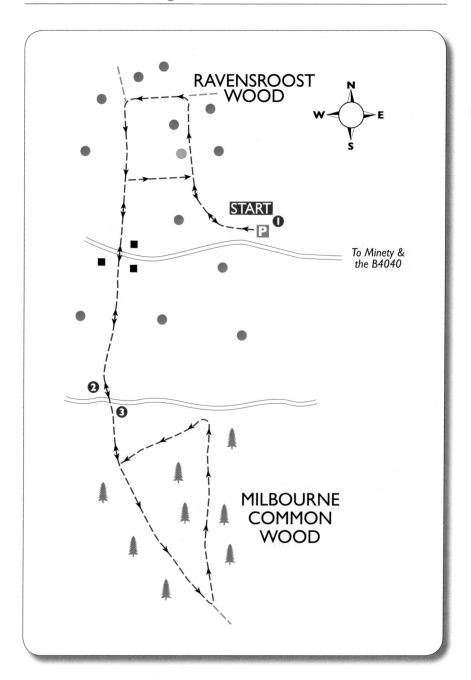

RAVENSROOST
WOOD

START

To Minety &
the B4040

MILBOURNE
COMMON
WOOD

In ½ mile, at the bottom of a slope, pass through a gap by a wooden barrier on the left – there is a broken footpath sign on the right. Follow this footpath for 500 yards until it emerges into a wide open space a little way before a lane. At this point, follow a footpath on the left back into the woodland for 350 yards back to **Blackberry Lane**. Retrace your steps to the right, back up to a quiet lane.

3 Cross over and follow the byway opposite for ¼ mile back to another quiet lane. Follow the byway opposite for 250 yards to a pair of white stones on the right and a barrier at the entrance to **Ravensroost Wood**, ignoring an earlier entrance marked by a stile. Follow the path ahead for 200 yards to the former shooting hut. Either retrace your steps to the right back to the car park or follow the path ahead to the edge of the woodland, turn right and follow a faint little-used path back to the car park.

2

Barbury Castle and Smeathe's Ridge

Fantastic views from the top of Barbury Castle ramparts.

Each major town has its 'playground' and the Barbury Castle Country Park fulfils this role for Swindon. This Iron Age hillfort sits high on the Marlborough Downs, where the escarpment drops away to the flatlands of north Wiltshire and more distant Berkshire, encompassing the Upper Thames Valley and the Vale of the White Horse. The walk heads out along Smeathe's Ridge, wonderful open country with views that border onto some horse gallops that are far enough away not to bother dogs. The return is by way of enclosed tracks that run through the clay vale, before a climb onto Burderop Down where we find a memorial stone to Alfred Williams and Richard Jefferies, two local writers who were inspired by this downland landscape. Williams described, 'The joy found in every hill and hollow and the company in solitude'. Jefferies wrote that, 'It is eternity now and I am in the midst of it; it is about me in the sunshine'. These words will no doubt be lost on our four-footed friends, who will simply revel in the chance to run free in this vast open landscape.

Terrain
This walk follows tracks across the Marlborough Downs and the clay vale below. There is one ascent towards journey's end onto Burderop Down, but it is nothing too challenging.

Where to park
The Barbury Castle Country Park car park (GR: 156762). **Map**: OS Explorer 157 Marlborough & Savernake Forest.

How to get there
Three miles south of Swindon, the A361 Devizes road passes through Wroughton. At the mini-roundabout in the centre of the village, follow the signs for the Barbury Castle Country Park. Four miles from Wroughton, at the top of a steep hill, the lane ends in the Country Park parking area.

Refreshments
Barbury Castle Country Park has many excellent spots for a picnic. The dog-friendly White Hart in Wroughton serves food and has two beautiful gardens that are perfect for families. ☎ 01793 812436. **Postcode**: SN4 9JX.

Dog factors
. . . .
Distance: 5½ miles.
Road walking: Very short sections of road walking near the car park.
Livestock: Very occasionally there are cattle in a field where the track drops down from Smeathe's Ridge. **Note**: There is a shooting club near the end of the walk. If your dog is afraid of the sound of gunshot, an 'out and back' walk along Smeathe's Ridge is an excellent alternative.
Stiles: None.
Nearest vets: Drove Veterinary Hospital, 252 Croft Road, Swindon SN1 4RW. ☎ 01793 522483

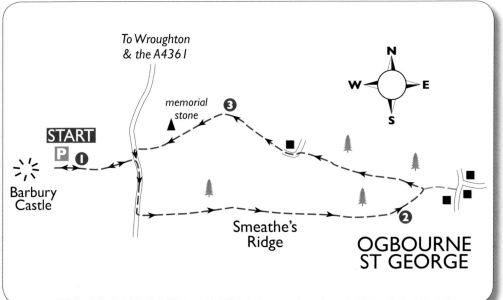

A brief pause to catch his breath.

The Walk

1 Walk back out of the car park and follow a lane to the right. Having passed **Ridgeway Farm** and a riding complex, pass through a gate on the left and follow the **Ridgeway** across the hilltop, with horse gallops on the left. In 1¼ miles, pass through a gate and continue following the **Ridgeway** ahead across a second field.

2 After ¼ mile, by a marker post, keep on the path as it veers left towards a gate in the end field boundary. Follow the **Ridgeway** across two more fields to a junction and turn left to follow a signposted bridleway. In just under 1 mile, at a junction, follow a farm road to the left, initially passing a stand of conifers. In ¾ mile, at the next junction, walk ahead for a few paces before veering left onto a path that climbs uphill to reach a junction.

3 Follow the left-hand path that winds its way around to a handgate, cross the field ahead to another gate and follow the path uphill to a clump of trees on **Burderop Hill**. Continue following the path across the hilltop, passing a memorial stone to Richard Jefferies and Alfred Williams, to reach a gate and road. Turn left and, in 100 yards, right, back into the **Barbury Castle car park**.

Castle Combe

Finn on top of West Yatton Down.

Most **visitors to Castle Combe experience** a sense of déjà vu, with the village seeming all too familiar. This is because it has featured on calendars and jigsaw puzzles, in guidebooks and even on the big screen, being one of Britain's most picturesque villages. The film in question, incidentally, was the 1967 version of *Doctor Doolittle*. The By Brook winds its way through the village, passing beneath a triple-arch bridge at the bottom of the main street, with handsome cottages of mellowed limestone pressing onto the road. Away from the village, the local landscape is quite exceptional, with the unimproved limestone grassland of West Yatton Down being home to a rich array of flora and fauna. There is also a section of the By Brook

Valley, where wooded hillsides come tumbling down to the banks of arguably the Bristol Avon's most delightful tributary stream, that flows from its source above Castle Combe through Ford, Slaughterford and Box to its confluence with the Avon at Bathford. Other than a few sections of road-walking near Castle Combe itself, where leads will be necessary, dogs will enjoy running free in what is a most picturesque part of the southern Cotswolds.

Terrain
A mix of woodland paths and fields, with the occasional quiet lane. There are a couple of climbs between Long Dean and Castle Combe, both of which are relatively short and not too challenging.

Where to park
The visitors' car park in Upper Castle Combe (GR: 846777). **Map**: OS Explorer 156 Chippenham & Bradford-on-Avon.

How to get there
The B4039 runs from the A420 west of Chippenham, through Yatton Keynell before reaching Upper Castle Combe, where the car park is clearly signposted.

Refreshments
The White Hart in Castle Combe is a dog-friendly pub with a lovely courtyard and garden where dogs can relax in the sun. The pub is open from 11 am until 11 pm every day, and food is served all day. ☎ 01249 782295. **Postcode**: SN14 7HT.

Dog factors

Distance: 5 miles.
Road walking: There are short sections of walking on quiet lanes near Castle Combe. More significant is a 300 yard section of verge-walking alongside the B4039 between Castle Combe and West Yatton Down where dogs will have to be on their leads.
Livestock: There can be cattle in the fields before West Yatton Down.
Stiles: There are a couple of stiles on the hilltop above Long Dean, both alongside farm gates.
Nearest vets: Garden Veterinary Group, 1 Bristol Road, Chippenham SN15 1NQ. ☎ 01249 653181

Wiltshire – A Dog Walker's Guide

The Walk

. . . .

1 Leave the car park, turn left up to the **B4039**, turn left and, in 40 yards, take the right turn signposted to **Grittleton**. In ¼ mile, at a crossroads, turn right onto a byway. Follow this byway for just over ½ mile to a junction, follow the road ahead for 40 yards and, where it bears right, keep ahead along a byway. In 600 yards, join the **B4039** and follow a verge on the right for 300 yards before turning right by a gateway to follow a bridleway.

2 Having passed a cottage and gateway, continue along an enclosed path to reach a pair of farm gates. Pass through the left-hand gateway and follow a path ahead, initially passing underneath some power cables. Beyond the next gate, continue through woodland to the next gate before walking ahead across a field to reach a gateway in the far right corner of the field. Continue

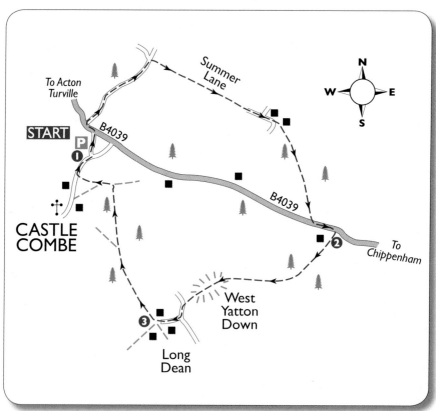

A leisurely swan has By Brook to itself.

through woodland for ¼ mile to reach a gate and a valley known as **West Yatton Down**, an area of unimproved limestone grassland. Walk through this valley, keeping to the right of the trees in the valley bottom, before bearing left in 350 yards to reach a gate and lane. Turn left and, in a few paces, right along a cul de sac lane that leads down into **Long Dean**.

③ In 250 yards, at a junction by a post box, turn right and follow a track past **Rose Cottage** that climbs out of the hamlet. In ¾ mile, where the path emerges into an open hillside field, take the path that veers right uphill to reach a handgate and woodland. Follow the path through the woodland for ½ mile to reach a wooden barrier and track. Turn left for a few paces before turning left onto a footpath that drops downhill to reach the road in **Castle Combe**. Turn left to explore the village, or turn right and follow the road uphill for 350 yards before turning left back to the car park.

4

Box Hill and the Hazelbury Estate

Looking down on Box.

The **Quarrymans Arms on Box Hill** has its origins in the local stone mining industry. Once the local for hundreds of Bath-stone miners who worked under this hillside, today the Quarrymans Arms has become a popular destination in its own right. Its reputation is built on decent food and well kept real ales – not to mention the fine views and mining-related memorabilia. The pub comes at journey's end after a walk across open hilltops with fine views. From Box Hill Common, the first highlight is an area of ancient woodland, whose pitted ground is evidence of a stone-mining past. Beyond the tree cover, the path emerges onto open ground with a fine view

Dog factors

Distance: 3½ miles.
Road walking: There are very short sections of road walking at the start and finish of the walk in Box Hill, albeit on quiet unclassified roads.
Livestock: All of the fields along the way are arable. There can be pigs near Hazelbury Common.
Stiles: None.
Nearest vets: Hale Veterinary Group, 37 High Street, Corsham SN13 0EZ. ☎ 01249 715097

across the By Brook Valley and Box to Colerne on the distant hilltop. More woodland follows – watch out for the pigs running free here – before the walk reaches Hazelbury Common. An oasis of natural grassland, this common is home to a rich variety of flora and fauna; 31 species of butterfly have been recorded on the common including Clouded Yellow, Small Blue and Comma. A rather grand driveway brings the route to Hazelbury Manor, whose most spectacular features are the hall bay and the two-storey porch, before open fields return the walk to Box Hill.

Terrain

A mix of field margins, enclosed footpaths and wide tracks. There is one ascent along the way but it is far from challenging.

Where to park

There are parking spaces on the edge of Box Hill Common (GR: 834693).
Map: OS Explorer 156 Chippenham & Bradford-on-Avon.

How to get there

Leave the A365 Box to Melksham road at Fiveways Junction, 1 mile from Box, and follow the B3109 towards Corsham. In 1 mile, turn left into White Ennox Lane. In 600 yards, at a crossroads by Tunnel Inn, turn left and drive for 350 yards to a junction by a small green. Turn right at this junction to reach Box Hill Common in 50 yards.

Refreshments

The Quarrymans Arms on Box Hill, almost at the end of the walk, welcomes dogs in its bar area. It is open seven days a week, serving food until 3 pm and between 5:30 pm and 9 pm on weekdays. At weekends, food is served all day until 9 pm. ☎ 01225 743569. **Postcode**: SN13 8HN.

Wide open spaces to explore.

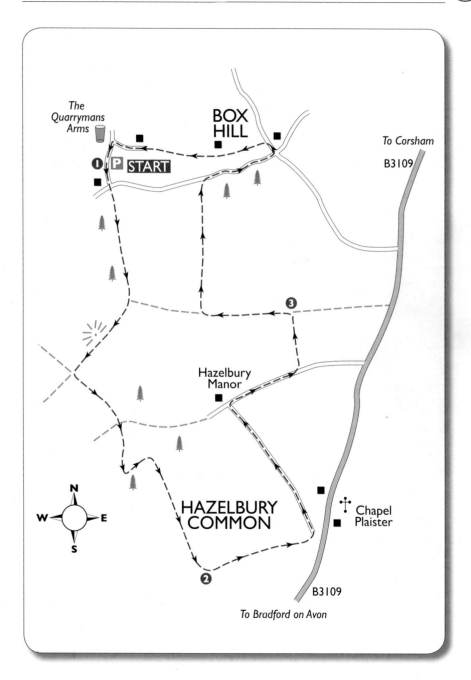

The Walk

. . . .

1 Walk back to the junction and follow the road that runs to the right of the green. Cross the road and follow a bridleway into woodland, keeping left at an early fork. Follow the path along the edge of the woodland for 350 yards until it bears left out of the tree cover. In a few steps, at a junction, take the path on the right that runs along the edge of the hilltop, with fine views down to the village of **Box**. In 350 yards, at a junction just past the end of a wall, follow the track to the left. Drop down to a crossroads in 300 yards before following the track opposite that climbs uphill to reach **Hazelbury Common** in ¼ mile.

2 Turn left and walk up the left edge of the common to reach a driveway on the left leading to **Hazelbury Manor**, just before the B3109 road. Walk down the driveway and, in 500 yards, immediately past a pair of stone gateposts, turn right along an estate road. Pass a barn on the left in 200 yards before continuing for another 200 yards to a point where a footpath crosses the estate road. Turn left and walk across the middle of a field to a gap in a stone wall opposite.

3 Beyond this gap, turn left and walk along the edge of the next field for 350 yards before turning right to walk across the open field towards a copse opposite. Pass through a gate by this copse before following a road to the right to a crossroads by **Tunnel Inn**. Turn left and, in 40 yards by a property, turn left onto an enclosed footpath. Keeping right at a fork, follow this path for 200 yards until it emerges by some properties. Keep ahead on an access road to a fork by **Sidan Cottage** and veer right to emerge on the road in **Box Hill** by the **Quarrymans Arms**. Turn left back to the common.

5

Bradford on Avon and Avoncliff

Some careful steering of the narrowboats at Avoncliff.

I n countless surveys, **Bradford on Avon** appears as one of Britain's finest small towns. Serried ranks of former weavers' cottages line the hillside above the River Avon, where the town bridge with its lock-up replaced what was formerly a 'broad ford'. Water is a feature in the town, with the Kennet and Avon Canal also passing this way. The walk follows a section of the canal and a woodland path through to neighbouring Avoncliff, where the canal crosses the Avon by way of one of the finest aqueducts in southern Britain. There is also the Cross Guns Inn, with its terraced garden dropping down to the banks of the Avon, a magical spot that has made the place a magnet for visitors. A riverside path brings the walk back into Bradford on Avon, and such is the popularity of the area with dog walkers, man's best friend will no doubt arrive home having made numerous new friends.

Dog factors

Distance: 3 miles.
Road walking: There is a short section of road walking on a quiet lane from Becky Addy Wood down into Avoncliff. The canal towpath is popular with cyclists.
Livestock: There are occasionally sheep in the fields between the Kennet and Avon Canal and Becky Addy Wood.
Stiles: None.
Nearest vets: Harris Hill and Gibbons Veterinary Surgery, Prospect House, Bradford on Avon, Wiltshire BA15 1LA. ☎ 01225 862656

Terrain
A flat and easy walk with one gentle climb up to Becky Addy Wood, where the woodland path can be rough underfoot.

Where to park
Park in the station car park in Bradford on Avon (GR: 825607). **Map:** OS Explorer 156 Chippenham & Bradford-on-Avon.

How to get there
Bradford on Avon lies on the A363 that runs from the A4 at Bathford through to Trowbridge. The railway station is in the centre of the town, on the Trowbridge side of the Town Bridge. The station is clearly signposted.

Refreshments

The Cross Guns in Avoncliff is a dog-friendly pub that even sells snacks for your four-footed friend. The pub is open all day every day, with food being served between 12 noon and 9 pm. Back in Bradford on Avon, there is open grassland by the river that is ideal for a picnic, with a nearby shallow stretch of river for water-loving dogs.

The Walk

① Walk to the far end of the station car park and follow a path to the left signposted to the **Tithe Barn** and **Avoncliff**, that initially passes under a railway bridge. Follow the path across a park before veering left on a gravel path up to the **Kennet and Avon Canal**. Follow the towpath to the right and, in ½ mile, either continue along the towpath to **Avoncliff**, or (as shown on the map here) cross a footbridge over the canal and follow a path on the far bank along to a gate and hillside field. Walk along the bottom right edge of this field to a gate before climbing uphill in a second field to a gate at the entrance to **Becky Addy Wood**. Follow the path through the woodland, keeping left at a fork, to reach a lane in ¼ mile.

② Follow this lane to the right downhill into **Avoncliff**, keeping on the road as it bears right by the entrance to a property called **Ancliff Square**. Descend some steps to pass under **Avoncliff Aqueduct**, then walk up to the **Cross**

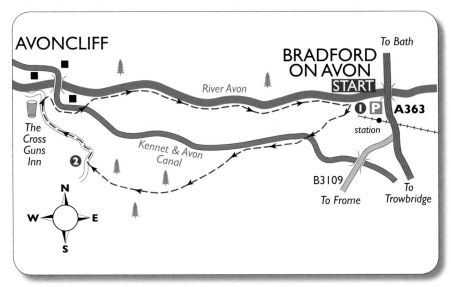

Finn checking out the picnic spot.

Guns Inn before bearing right up to the canal. Follow the towpath to the left towards **Bradford on Avon** for 200 yards before following a path on the left that drops downhill to the **River Avon**. Follow the Avon upstream for ¾ mile across 2 fields then along a surfaced path for ½ mile back to the park in Bradford on Avon passed at the start of the walk. Cross this park and pass under the railway bridge to return to the station car park.

Morgan's Hill and the Wansdyke

Finn having a rest on the Wansdyke.

This walk onto the North Wessex Downs heads off from the Smallgrain picnic area, which was, unbelievably, a scrapyard until 1971. The name Smallgrain, incidentally, is thought to be a derogatory term for an unproductive area of poor soil. Morgan's Hill, the next port of call along the way, is an area of unimproved chalk grassland whose rich array of flora and

Dog factors

Distance: 5½ miles.
Road walking: None.
Livestock: There are occasionally sheep or cattle in the field beyond the Morgan's Hill Nature Reserve.
Stiles: None.
Nearest vets: The Hale Veterinary Group, Bank Row, Church Street, Calne, Wiltshire SN11 0SG. ☎ 01249 815563

fauna has earned the site a SSSI designation. Look out for the various species of orchid, as well as milkwort, vetch and the round-headed rampion, flora that in turn attracts as many as 20 different types of butterfly, including the Chalkhill Blue and the Duke of Burgundy. Morgan's Hill is bordered by the Wansdyke, a linear frontier of ditch and bank that was built by the Britons to act as a defence against invading pagan Saxons. History appears yet again in the form of a Roman road that ran from Mildenhall to Bath, a route that was significant for military logistics between the 1st and 5th centuries AD, and subsequently served as a drovers' track in the Middle Ages. All of this will be lost on our four-footed friends, however, who will simply revel in the chance to run off-lead on open grassland and along ancient tracks.

Terrain
An undulating landscape with no significant ascents or descents. There are fine open views across the downland along the way, on a walk that follows mainly enclosed tracks, as well as stretches of open grassland.

Where to park
Park in the Smallgrain Plantation picnic area between Calne and Devizes (GR: 019672). **Map:** OS Explorer 157 Marlborough & Savernake Forest.

How to get there

Leave the A4 two miles east of Calne town centre and follow an unclassified road signposted to Bishops Cannings. In 1¾ miles, at the top of a climb, turn left into the Smallgrain Plantation picnic area.

Refreshments

There are no pubs or cafés on or close to this walk. The Smallgrain Plantation car park, however, borders an open area of grassland with picnic tables, the perfect place to stop and linger awhile with a picnic at journey's end.

Straight walking on the Roman road.

Wiltshire – A Dog Walker's Guide

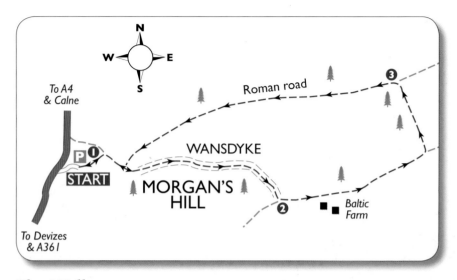

The Walk

. . . .

1 Walk to the far end of the car park, climb some steps and drop down to a track that was originally the Roman road running from Mildenhall to Bath. Turn right and continue for 350 yards to a junction by a **Morgan's Hill Reserve information board**. Pass through a handgate on the right and ahead is a bank and ditch that marks the course of the **Wansdyke**. Follow the **Wansdyke** across 4 fields to reach a small copse in 1 mile.

2 Pass through this copse to join a track. Turn left and follow this track for 1 mile across open countryside to a pair of metal farm gates and a track on the left. Turn left and keep to this track until you come to a belt of trees, walking in the direction of the **Cherhill Monument** on the distant skyline.

3 In ½ mile, just past this belt of trees, join the track that marks the course of the Roman road. Follow this track for 1 ½ miles back to the information board at the entrance to the **Morgan's Hill Reserve**, passed near the start of the walk. Retrace your steps along the main track for 350 yards to some steps on the left that lead back to the car park.

Roundway Down

Finn admiring the downland escarpment.

Roundway Hill stands at the divide between the chalk hills of the North Wessex Downs and the Bristol Avon's clay vale. The views from this lofty hilltop perch are immense, encompassing not only the Avon Vale, but also the escarpment of Salisbury Plain and the more distant Cotswold Hills. The setting is made all the more atmospheric by the presence of Oliver's Castle, an enclosed site of 3½ acres protected by just a single rampart, and overlooked by a number of isolated beech trees that attract encircling rooks and crows. The open downland may appear as just peaceful countryside in this day and age but had you been walking this way in 1643, you would soon have been diving for cover. This is Roundway Down, scene all those years ago of an English Civil War battle. It was here that Sir William Waller and his Parliamentary troops were attacked by Royalist forces. Sir William fled the site, endowing it with the name 'Runaway Hill' – later to become the Roundway as it is known today. As for dogs – they will simply love the vast open spaces and car-free tracks where they can run free.

Terrain
A flat and open landscape, crossed by a network of tracks and bridleways. There is also a section of woodland walking in Roundway Hill Covert.

Where to park
The Leipzig Plantation car park on Roundway Down (GR: 014642). **Map:** OS Explorer 157 Marlborough & Savernake Forest.

How to get there
One mile north-east of Devizes on the A361 road to Swindon, a left turn leads to the village of Roundway. In ½ mile, turn right onto a cul de sac by a telephone box and climb uphill towards Roundway Hill. In 600 yards, keep right at a fork on a road leading to Leipzig Plantation. In 200 yards, having passed the plantation, park on the left alongside a track leading out onto Roundway Down.

Dog factors
· ·

Distance: 5 miles.
Road walking: There is a short section of road walking by Hill Cottage but, given this is an access road only, you will be unlucky if you encounter any vehicles.
Livestock: None.
Stiles: None.
Nearest vets: Estcourt Vets, 5 Estcourt Street, Devizes, Wiltshire SN10 1LQ. ☎ 01380 723687

Refreshments

The open grassland of Roundway Hill, with its fine views across the Avon Vale, is quite the most perfect spot for a picnic. In Devizes, The Black Swan offers a dog-friendly welcome. This 18th-century coaching inn serves freshly prepared food daily with homemade cakes served at the bar. ☎ 01380 698070. **Postcode**: SN10 1JQ

The Walk

. . . .

❶ Follow the track to the left onto **Roundway Down**. After 1¼ miles, at a crossroads, turn left. When you come to a junction in ¾ mile by **Hill Cottage**, continue ahead for ½ mile to the second track going off on the left, signposted as a bridleway – the first left turn is a byway.

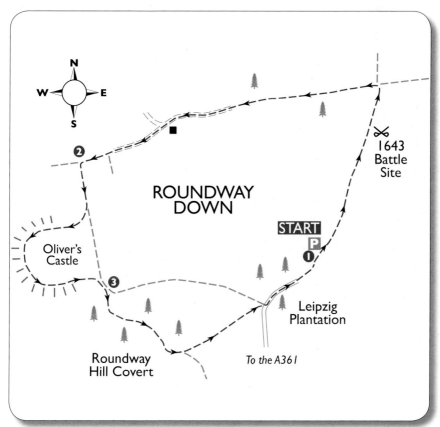

There's lots to explore under the trees.

❷ In 350 yards, turn right by a bridleway/footpath sign. Follow the footpath ahead, with a fence on the left, along to a gate before bearing left to follow a path along the edge of the escarpment to some beech trees by the ramparts of **Oliver's Castle**. On reaching the south-western corner of the hillfort, follow the path as it bears left, with the path still running along the edge of the escarpment. In 300 yards, beyond a gate, turn right into a parking area.

❸ Pass through a gate in the corner of this parking area to enter **Roundway Hill Covert**. Keeping left at an early junction, follow a path that runs along the eastern boundary of the woodland. After ¾ mile, at the end of the woodland, bear left to a gate and open field. Cross the field ahead to a gate opposite before keeping ahead on a grassy path that runs across to **Leipzig Plantation**. Follow the path through this area of woodland back to the parking area.

Ancient Avebury

Silbury Hill is a prehistoric artifical chalk mound.

World Heritage status is not earned lightly and is awarded by UNESCO on the basis of being of 'outstanding universal value'. In the case of Avebury this also involves 'bearing unique testimony to civilisations that have disappeared'. The civilisations in question are the Neolithic and Bronze Age peoples. The sites are many and extend beyond the well-known stone circle with its bank and ditch; there is a fine stone avenue, any number of barrows, the mysterious mound that is Silbury Hill and Britain's oldest road in the shape of the Ridgeway. It is also the setting that makes Avebury so unique, with the village surrounded by Wiltshire's open chalk downland, wide open spaces with big skies and far-ranging vistas. Almost the entire walk is off lead, with field margins and the occasional copse to sniff about in, so you will have a tired and happy hound by the end of the day.

Dog factors

Distance: 6 miles.
Road walking: The A4361 has to be crossed at the start of the walk, as does the B4003 one mile further on. Dogs should be kept on their leads in Avebury at the end of the walk. Be aware that the Ridgeway can be used by motorcycles and 4 by 4 vehicles from 1st May to 30th September.
Livestock: Sheep often graze within the confines of Avebury's stone circle.
Stiles: None.
Nearest vets: Macqueen Veterinary Centre, 1 Waller Road, Hopton Park, Devizes, SN10 2GH. ☎ 01380 728505

Terrain

A mix of field margins, enclosed footpaths and wide tracks. There are a couple of moderate ascents along the way, but these bring rewards in the form of wide, expansive views across some of Wiltshire's finest downland.

Where to park

There is a signposted National Trust car park on the southern edge of Avebury, fee payable but free to NT members. (GR: 099697). **Map**: OS Explorer 157 Marlborough & Savernake Forest.

How to get there

Avebury lies one mile north of the A4 at Beckhampton on the A4361 road to Swindon.

Refreshments

The Red Lion in the centre of Avebury, passed at the end of the walk, welcomes dogs in the front bar or outside on leads. It is open seven days a week with food served from 11 am until 10 pm. ☎ 01672 539266. **Postcode**: SN8 1RF.

The Walk

1 Leave the car park and turn right along the **A4361** for 25 yards before crossing over to enter a small enclosure opposite. Dogs can now come off their leads. Pass through a handgate at the end of this enclosure and follow an enclosed path for 600 yards alongside the infant **River Kennet** to reach a footbridge on the right and a path leading to **Silbury Hill**. Ignoring this path, continue ahead for 200 yards to reach a gate and open field.

2 Turn left and follow a permissive path that climbs to the top of **Waden Hill** before descending to reach a gate in the bottom corner of the field at the entrance to the **Avenue**. Turn right and follow the bottom of the field – another permissive path – to reach a handgate on the left in 350 yards. Cross the **B4003** – dogs briefly back on their leads – to a handgate opposite and follow another permissive path over to the far right corner of the field ahead. Beyond another handgate, follow a grassy path that climbs uphill to a pair of tumuli, covered in beech trees.

A fine day at the world famous prehistoric Avebury stone circle.

3 Continue following the path uphill to a junction by another tumulus and beeches. Turn right and walk for 150 yards to a junction with the **Ridgeway**. Turn left and follow the **Ridgeway** for 1¼ miles to a junction, with **Fyfield Down** on the right. Turn left and follow a track – it becomes a lane beyond **Manor Farm** – for 1½ miles to reach the **A4361** in **Avebury**, with dogs back on their leads as you approach the village. Cross over, passing the **Red Lion** on the right, to join **Avebury's High Street**. In 100 yards, having passed the **Henge Shop** and a section of the stone circle on the left, turn left along a path that leads back to the car park

Ogbourne St Andrew

Picture-perfect Ogbourne village.

A **'bourne' is an intermittent stream and,** in the case of Ogbourne St Andrew, this stream is the delightfully named 'River Og', that flows from its source near the hamlet of Draycot Foliat to its confluence with the Kennet at Marlborough. The local church was referred to by Pevsner as, 'Not big. Of flint except for the west tower'. Of rather more interest was reference to a bowl barrow in the churchyard, the site of pagan Saxon burials that yielded no fewer than twenty skeletons when excavated in 1885. Quiet byways and tracks take the walk up onto hilltops above the village, shown on

Dog factors

Distance: 5 miles.
Road walking: Short sections of road walking in Ogbourne St Andrew at the start and finish of the walk, where the busy A346 has to be crossed twice. A short stretch of quiet cul de sac lane is followed on the hilltop above the village.
Livestock: None.
Stiles: None.
Nearest vets: Riverside Veterinary Centre, London Road, Marlborough SN8 2AG. ☎ 01672 514875

the OS Explorer map as Poulton Downs, where dogs will enjoy running free along traffic-free bridleways with far-ranging views. There is also a section of the 'Chiseldon & Marlborough Railway Path' that follows the former trackbed of what is known as 'Swindon's Other Railway'. This is part of the longer 'Midland and South Western Junction Railway' that originally ran from Cheltenham, through Swindon and Marlborough, and on to Southampton. Closed to passenger traffic in 1961, the path is today a shared-use route for walkers and cyclists and, being popular with dog walkers, there will be any number of sights, smells and sounds to keep your pooch amused.

Terrain

The walk is largely along enclosed tracks and footpaths, with a few short sections of quiet lanes. There is one moderate climb onto Poulton Downs, with a gentle descent on the return to Ogbourne St Andrew.

Where to park

On the roadside outside the church in Ogbourne St Andrew (GR 189724). **Map**: OS Explorer 157 Marlborough & Savernake Forest.

How to get there

Take the A346 from Marlborough heading north towards Swindon. In 2 miles, in the village of Ogbourne St Andrew, turn left into a lane by the war memorial. In 250 yards, by a small green, turn left and park by the church.

Refreshments

On the A346 heading towards Ogbourne St George is the dog-friendly Inn with the Well where food is served from 12 noon to 2:30 pm and 6:30 pm until 8:30 pm each day, other than Monday and Thursday lunchtimes.
☎ 01672 841445

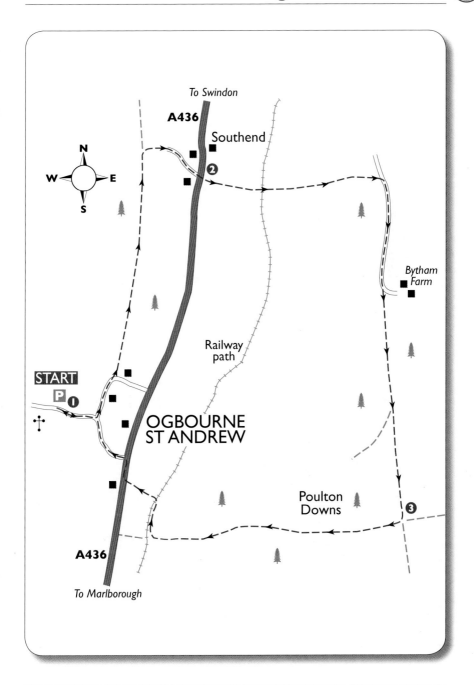

Wiltshire – A Dog Walker's Guide

The Walk

1 Return to the green and follow the road to the left. In 100 yards, where the road bears right by a bungalow, turn left onto a byway. Follow this byway for ¾ mile to a junction before turning right on the **'Ridgeway Byway'**. Follow this track – it becomes a lane – down to the **A346** in the hamlet of **Southend**.

A perfect walk for all shapes and sizes.

② Cross the main road and follow the **Ridgeway Byway** opposite for just over ½ mile to a quiet lane on the hilltop. Turn right and follow this lane for ¼ mile to a point where it bears left to **Bytham Farm**. Keep ahead at this point along a track to some woodland, pass through the woodland and, where the track emerges from the trees, keep right at a junction. Follow this track for 600 yards to a crossroads.

③ Turn right and, in just over 1 mile, a little way before the track reaches the **A346**, turn right onto the **Chiseldon and Marlborough Railway Path**. In 250 yards, just before reaching the rear of some properties, turn left down an unmetalled road to the **A346**. Turn right, walk past the **Silks on the Downs** to a **war memorial** and turn left onto a quiet side road. Follow this road for 200 yards around to a junction before turning left back to the church.

Milk Hill and Adam's Grave

Finn looking serious on the Wansdyke.

This walk lies entirely above the 700 ft contour line as it crosses perhaps the finest downland within North Wessex. The views are vast, with the greater part of the landscape unspoilt by modern farming techniques due to its Nature Reserve status. It is not just natural history, but also ancient history that features on this walk. Initially there is a section of the Wessex Ridgeway before our steps follow the Wansdyke, a linear frontier of bank and ditch, across the hilltop. A scattering of sarsen stones follows on Milk Hill, where the landscape is also dotted about with earthworks such as a cross dyke. The walk passes quite literally above the Alton Barnes White Horse before climbing onto one final hilltop where the earthworks mark the remains of Adam's Grave, a late-Neolithic long barrow. Dogs will love this walk, with the entire route being off road and across open grassland where they can run free.

Dog factors
· ·

Distance: 3½ miles.
Road walking: Other than crossing a road at the start and finish from the car park, there is no road walking.
Livestock: Sheep often graze in one of the fields between the Wansdyke and the Alton Barnes White Horse.
Stiles: None.
Nearest vets: Belmont House Veterinary Surgery, Salisbury Road Business Park, Salisbury Road, Pewsey SN9 5PZ. ☎ 01672 563413

Terrain

This walk crosses open hilltops, with one gentle climb up to the Wansdyke at the start and a short, sharp climb to Adam's Grave near the end. The route follows tracks and fieldpaths with fine views at every turn.

Where to park

There is a car park on the hilltop above the village of Alton Barnes for visitors to this part of the North Wessex Downs (GR: 117638). **Map:** OS Explorer 157 Marlborough & Savernake Forest.

How to get there

An unclassified road leaves the A361 north of Devizes and heads across the Vale of Pewsey to the A345 in Pewsey itself. At a crossroads in Alton Barnes, turn left and drive uphill onto the Downs. In one mile, at the top of a climb, turn right into a parking area below Knap Hill which is on the right.

Refreshments

There are no refreshment facilities on the walk, but the open ground around Adam's Grave is perfect for a picnic. Alternatively, follow the road back down into Alton Barnes and follow the signs for the Barge Inn on the Kennet and Avon Canal at Honeystreet. This quite excellent waterside pub is dog-friendly, quirky and atmospheric and claims to be, 'probably the most famous pub in the universe'. The Barge is open all day, every day. ☎ 01672 851705. **Postcode**: SN9 5PS.

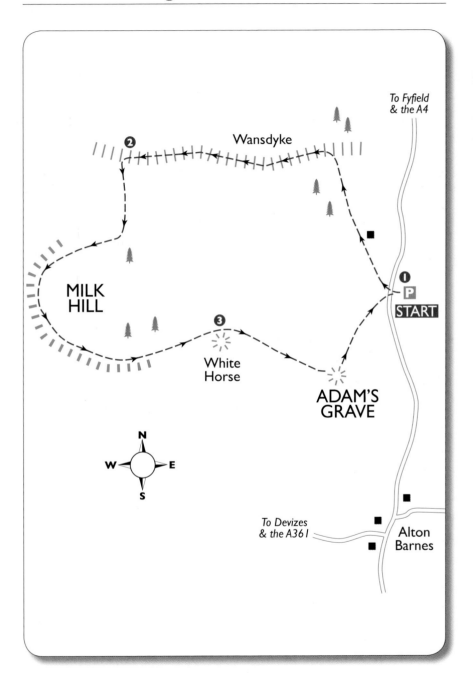

The Walk

· ·

1 Cross the road from the car park, pass through a handgate opposite, and turn right to follow a byway along the right edge of 4 fields to reach the **Wansdyke Path** on the hilltop in just over ½ mile. Turn left and follow this path across the hilltop for 1 mile to reach a handgate on the left and a **Pewsey Downs National Nature Reserve** information board.

2 Pass through this gate and follow a well-defined grassy path across the left edge of 2 fields. In a third field, continue following this path as it passes to the right of a belt of trees. At the far end of the third field, keep on the path as it bears around to the left, keeping below the trees and always walking along the edge of the hilltop to reach the **Alton Barnes White Horse.**

3 Continue along the path for ½ mile to a prominent hilltop that is the location of **Adam's Grave**, an ancient long barrow. From this hilltop, drop down to a footpath that then crosses 3 fields to reach the clearly visible car park alongside the road below.

Open rolling landscape is perfect for energetic dogs.

Savernake Forest

Savernake's Grand Avenue makes for easy walking whatever the weather.

Savernake Forest extends for over 2,300 acres across an undulating plateau high above Marlborough. Prior to the Conquest, the forest embraced a much larger slice of Wiltshire countryside, and was a noted royal hunting ground. To this day, herds of roe and fallow deer still roam in the deeper parts of Savernake. From the centre of the forest, eight fine avenues of beech trees radiate outwards, following a design attributed to Capability Brown, the grandest of which is the three-mile-long Grand Avenue. Dogs will love running free in this woodland, with any number of interesting sights and smells. There will inevitably be other dogs out walking in Savernake, too, so there is the chance for your pooch to make some new friends.

Terrain
This is a flat and easy walk that follows woodland tracks and paths.

Where to park
The Postern Hill picnic area on the north-western corner of Savernake Forest (GR: 199680). **Map**: OS Explorer 157 Marlborough & Savernake Forest.

How to get there
Follow the A346 south from Marlborough. In 1 mile, turn left into the Postern Hill campsite and picnic area. At an early fork, keep right on the road leading to the picnic and barbecue area. In 100 yards, park on the right-hand side just before the picnic area.

Refreshments
There are no pubs or cafés on this walk but the car park borders a picnic area where you can also bring your own barbecues. Dogs would love the smell and taste of sausages, bacon and beef! The idyllic village of Wootton Rivers is just 4 miles to the south. The 16th-century thatched Royal Oak is dog friendly with outside seating and serves food daily. ☎ 01672 810322. **Postcode**: SN8 4NQ.

Dog factors
. . . .
Distance: 3½ miles.
Road walking: None, but look out for vehicles on the short section of the Grand Avenue.
Livestock: There could be deer in the more remote parts of the forest.
Stiles: None.
Nearest vets: Riverside Veterinary Centre, London Road, Marlborough SN8 2AG. ☎ 01672 514875

Wiltshire – A Dog Walker's Guide

The Walk

. . . .

1 Continue following the road into **Savernake Forest**, initially passing a toilet block on the left. In 100 yards, on reaching a wooden barrier, continue along a gravelled track that soon bears right and walk for 600 yards to a barrier and crossroads. Turn left and follow a track shown on the OS map as **'White Road'**. Keep on this track, it bears left along the way, to a right turn in 600 yards immediately past a 'no through road' sign on the right – if you get as far as a wooden barrier beyond which is the A4, you have gone too far.

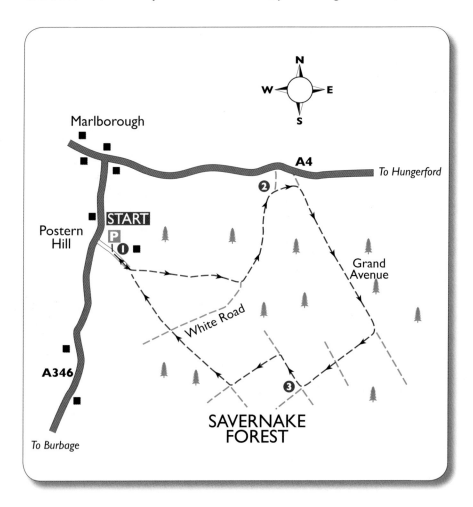

A shady forest glade.

2 Follow this path for 350 yards as it winds its way around to the **Grand Avenue**. Turn right and follow the **Grand Avenue** for 400 yards to a right turn by a wooden barrier. Take this right turn and, in 400 yards at a crossroads in a dip, continue ahead for 250 yards to reach the next crossroads, ignoring a slightly earlier right turn.

3 Turn right along a wide gravelled track and, in 350 yards, turn left at the next crossroads. After 250 yards, turn right at another crossroads and follow the path ahead for ¾ mile back to the picnic area and car park, passing **White Road Oak** at a junction along the way.

Great Bedwyn and Crofton

Lazy days by the Kennet and Avon Canal.

Crofton and Great Bedwyn lie just to the east of the Kennet and Avon Canal's summit pound. From here it is a steady descent to the Thames at Reading. At the summit level of any waterway, a reliable water supply is an absolute necessity. Literally hundreds of thousands of gallons of the precious liquid will be flowing out through the locks in both directions. The

Kennet and Avon's supply comes from Wilton Water, a reservoir, where steam engines at the nearby Crofton Pumping Station were originally used to raise the water to the actual summit level. This walk explores the fascinating canal-side environment in and around Crofton and Great Bedwyn, as well as taking in a fine stretch of countryside to the south-east of the canal. This includes Bedwyn Brail, an extensive area of mixed woodland; Wilton Windmill, high on a lonely hillside; and the village of Wilton itself, where the Swan Inn is a dog-friendly pub.

Dog factors

Distance: 5½ miles.
Road walking: ¾ mile of road walking in and around Wilton, mainly on a quiet lane.
Livestock: Ducks on the pond in Wilton.
Stiles: None.
Nearest vets: Riverside Veterinary Centre, London Road, Marlborough SN8 2AG. ☎ 01672 514875

Terrain

A mixture of canal towpath and fields, woodland tracks and quiet lanes that cross a gently undulating landscape.

Where to park

The River and Waterway's Trust car park by the Kennet and Avon Canal in Great Bedwyn (GR 281644). **Map:** OS Explorer 157 Marlborough & Savernake Forest.

How to get there

Leave the A4 four miles east of Marlborough and follow an unclassified road to Great Bedwyn. In the village, keep ahead at a junction by the Cross Keys, cross the railway line and the Kennet and Avon Canal before turning immediately right into a car park alongside the waterway.

Refreshments

The Swan at Wilton, halfway around the walk, is a dog-friendly pub. Food is served Monday to Friday between 12 noon and 3 pm and 6 pm and 9 pm. The kitchen is open until 2:30 pm on Saturdays, whilst on Sundays food is served between 12 noon and 3 pm. ☎ 01672 870274. **Postcode:** SN8 3SS.

Wiltshire – A Dog Walker's Guide

The Walk

1 From the car park, follow the towpath away from bridge 95 for just under 2 miles until **Wilton Water** appears on the left, with **Crofton Pumping Station** on the right. Turn left and follow a path that borders Wilton Water, the reservoir, on the right-hand side. After ½ mile, keep on the path as it veers right to leave an arable field to join a lane in **Wilton** by a duck pond.

2 Follow the road to the left along to the **Swan** in Wilton. Keep on the road that bears left by the inn, signposted to **Great Bedwyn**. In 350 yards, take what is the second right turn, signposted to **Wilton Windmill** and **Shalbourne**. Having passed the windmill on the right in 350 yards, continue for 350 yards

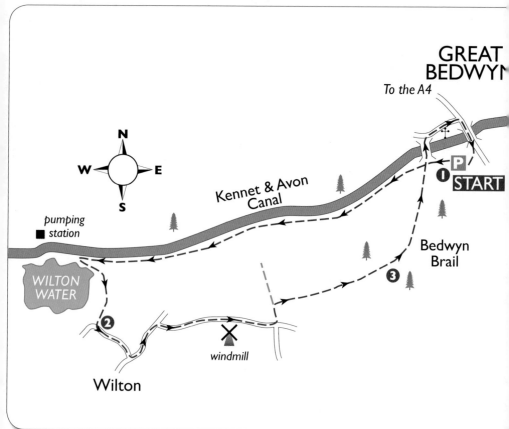

Wilton Windmill still produces stone-ground flour.

to a track on the left opposite a right turn to **Hungerford**. Turn left and after 200 yards, at a junction, turn right onto what soon becomes a grassy ride. Keep right at a junction in 150 yards on a path signposted to **Great Bedwyn** and, after a few paces, turn left into **Bedwyn Brail**.

3 In ¾ mile, what has been a gravelled track becomes a grassy ride. Ignore a path going off to the right and, in 25 yards, keep left at a fork to follow a path that drops downhill to enter woodland. On emerging from this woodland, follow the left edge of 2 fields down towards **Great Bedwyn**. Veer right at the bottom of the second field to join the canal towpath by **bridge 96**. Turn right to walk back to the car park.

West Lavington and Salisbury Plain

Spotting something on the horizon.

S alisbury Plain, a vast chalk plateau, covers some 300 square miles of Wiltshire's landscape. Half of the plain is owned by the Ministry of Defence, ownership of which has meant very limited access for the public and no cultivation or development. Ironically, this has made the area a wildlife haven with the plain being the largest area of unimproved chalk grassland in north-west Europe. This walk from West Lavington explores the fringes of this great wilderness, following a section of the Imber Range Perimeter Path. Imber is a deserted village in the heart of the plain, evacuated in 1943 with the residents given just 47 days' notice to leave their homes and never to return. The village was subsequently used by troops practising street fighting. Expect far-ranging views, not only across Salisbury Plain, but also to the north over the Vale of Pewsey towards the North Wessex Downs. It is a walk where dogs can run free and their owners can enjoy peace and solitude in a truly remote corner of the county.

Terrain

This walk follows enclosed footpaths and tracks with just a short section of road walking at the end. There are two hills along the way but the rewards are the fine views from the hilltops.

Where to park

The entrance to West Lavington Manor is on the eastern side of the A360 just south of the Churchill Arms. Opposite the manor is a side turning called White Street. In 40 yards, park on a gravelled area on the right where a footpath leaves the road. If this is full – there is room for about four vehicles – then in another 150 yards there is a small lay-by outside the local cemetery. (GR: 005532). **Map**: OS Explorer 130 Salisbury & Stonehenge.

How to get there

West Lavington lies on the A360 midway between Devizes and Shrewton.

Refreshments

The Churchill Arms lies on the A360 in West Lavington. This is a dog-friendly pub that also has a large garden for those warmer months of the year. Food is served from 12 noon to 3 pm on weekdays, 12 noon to 9 pm on Saturdays and 12 noon to 6 pm on Sundays. Being a Wadworth of Devizes pub, there is a fine choice of real ales including the flagship 6X brew. ☎ 01380 812287. **Postcode**: SN10 4JB

The Walk

· ·

1 Follow the footpath at the back of the parking area for 50 yards, pass through a gate on the right and continue following what is an enclosed path. In 150 yards, at the next junction, turn left along an enclosed path, the playing fields of **Dauntsey's School** on the right. After 600 yards, at a junction on the edge of some woodland, turn right. At the next junction in 250 yards, turn left and, ignoring one early right turn, follow the main track ahead as it climbs

A beautiful walk across patchwork fields.

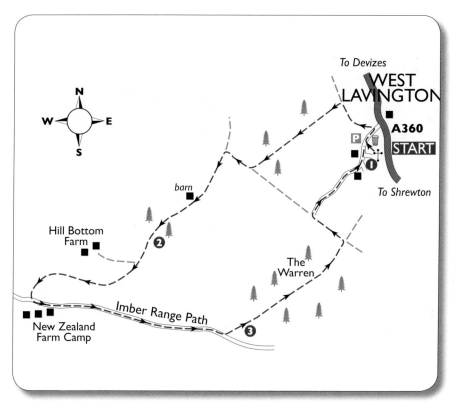

uphill, keeping ahead at a junction on the hilltop to pass a barn on the right. Continue following the grassy path ahead, keeping to the left of hedgerows so as to enjoy the far-ranging views.

2 In ½ mile, keep on the path as it drops downhill into a small copse. 50 yards beyond the copse, where the main gravelled track bears right, keep ahead on a grassy path. Continue along to some woodland, keep right along the edge of the woodland and beyond the last of the tree cover. Stay on the path as it bears left to climb uphill and reach the **Imber Range Perimeter Path** in 400 yards. Follow the road to the left across the hilltop, initially passing **New Zealand Farm Camp**, ignoring the private army road that veers off to the right initially. In just over 1 mile, turn left onto a byway – there is a sign – and head across to the left-hand of a pair of gaps in a line of conifer trees.

3 Follow the track downhill, passing through gateways, to reach some woodland in ½ mile. In 350 yards, at a crossroads at the end of the woodland, turn left

Dog factors

Distance: 6 miles.
Road walking: There is a short section of road walking at the end of the walk in West Lavington, albeit on a very quiet lane. The occasional vehicle appears on the Imber Range Perimeter Path but, given the open nature of the hilltop, any vehicle will be seen and heard long in advance.
Livestock: Cattle graze in the fields alongside the Imber Range Perimeter Path.
Stiles: None.
Nearest vets: The Paddock Veterinary Practice, Eastcroft Farm, Eastcott, Devizes SN10 4PJ. ☎ 01380 813202

and walk uphill to a crossroads in 300 yards. Turn right and follow a quiet lane downhill into **West Lavington**. In ½ mile, at the bottom of **Strawberry Hill**, turn left at a junction. After 40 yards, turn right at a junction down to the village church. Just before the church, bear left across to a footbridge and walk through a cemetery. At the end of the cemetery, turn left and walk up to some gates and a road. Turn right back to the parking area.

Corton and
Great Ridge Wood

Tree-topped barrows are characteristic of Wiltshire's ancient landscape.

Corton lies in the heart of the **Wylye Valley,** between Warminster and Salisbury, on the banks of a river that has been described as 'champagne flowing over gravel'. There is nothing along the way apart from sweeping downland and expansive views, huge areas of woodland and only the sounds of a natural landscape. There is not even a single habitation on a walk that is genuinely far from the proverbial madding crowd. The 'Great Ridge Wood' was referred to in W.H. Hudson's book *A Shepherd's Life* (1910), where he noted how the local villagers were allowed to take from it as much dead wood as they could find. Dogs will enjoy running free throughout this walk, and will find the sights, smells and sounds of the woodland section particularly intriguing.

Terrain
Well-defined tracks and woodland paths. One gentle climb into the Great Ridge Wood, but nothing that could be remotely described as strenuous.

Where to park
A small lay-by by the Dove Inn at Corton (GR 934405). **Map**: OS Explorer 143 Warminster & Trowbridge.

How to get there
From Warminster, an unclassified road runs in a south-easterly direction through the Wylye Valley, passing through Sutton Veny and Tytherington before reaching Corton. Just as you enter the village, veer left along a lane signposted to the Dove Inn and park almost immediately alongside a small green. Parking is limited to just 3 cars at this point so, if you have to park elsewhere, return to the green to start the walk.

Refreshments
Dogs are welcome in the bar area of the Dove Inn at Corton. The Dove offers first-class, modern pub food that is hearty, flavoursome and freshly prepared using the best of local ingredients. Open every day from 11 am, food is served between 12 noon and 2:30 pm and between 6 pm and 9 pm. ☎ 01985 850109. **Postcode**: BA12 0SZ

Dog factors

Distance: 7 miles.
Road walking: 400 yards of road walking at the start, albeit on a quiet lane. A farm access road on the hilltop that carries minimal traffic.
Livestock: None.
Stiles: None.
Nearest vets: Harris Hill and Gibbons Veterinary Surgery, Prospect House, Bradford on Avon, Wiltshire BA15 1LA. ☎ 01225 862656

The Walk

. . . .

1 Walk back up to the main road and turn right in the direction of **Warminster**. In ¼ mile, in a small beech copse, take the second of 2 consecutive paths on the left – a footpath rather than the restricted byway. After 250 yards, at a junction with a bridleway, turn left. Follow what is initially a grassy path – it becomes a gravel farm track – for 1½ miles to reach a gate and open field.

2 Follow the track across the right edge of this field as it climbs uphill to reach woodland in just under 1 mile. Ignoring side turns, follow the track ahead for 600 yards to reach a junction with a prominent gravel track. Turn left and follow this track for just over ½ mile to a junction where a prominent gravel

The Wylye, gently meandering through the countryside. This is a much prized trout stream though, so please don't let your dog go into the water!

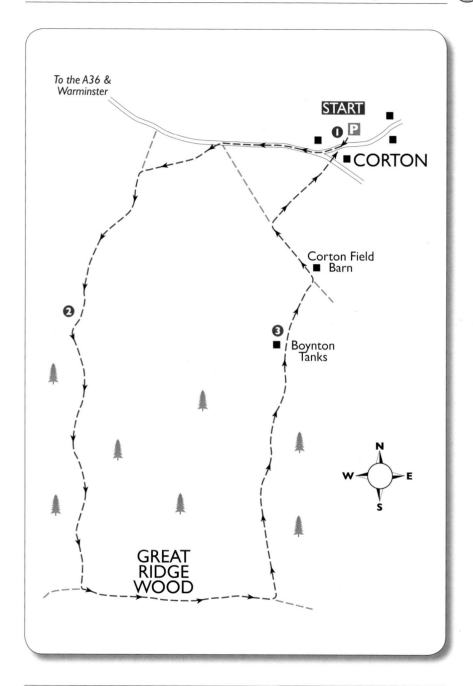

road goes off on the right, ignoring previous side turns. At this point, follow the **LEFT** turn to the next junction, ignore the track going off to the right and continue following the main road ahead until it reaches **Boynton Tanks**, a water facility.

3 Veer right into the trees at this point and follow a path that runs parallel to the main track down to a junction just above some farm buildings. Turn left – the buildings are shown on the OS map as **Corton Field Barn** – and follow what is a metalled lane for ¾ mile to a crossroads above a farm. Turn right for a few paces before veering left onto a side path that leaves the private farm road. After 250 yards, at a junction by **Foley's Cottage**, continue following the track opposite down to the main road in **Corton**. Turn left back to the junction by the green and the parking area.

The Stonehenge Estate

The origin of Stonehenge is estimated at 3100 BC and it is made with three different types of stone.

This walk is an altogether different take on the evocative landscape of Stonehenge. It explores the much wider Stonehenge Estate that includes barrows and tumuli, the Avenue and the Cursus, Woodhenge and Durrington Walls – ancient landmarks that are all too often missed in the standard tourist package. There is also the unforgettable site of Stonehenge itself, coming into view in the distance, as well as the approach by way of the Avenue that ancient peoples would once have trodden. This walk offers a magical experience at one of the world's greatest archaeological sites and, being traffic free, is just perfect as far as our four-footed friends are concerned.

Dog factors

Distance: 5 miles.
Road walking: None other than a very brief section at the start and finish of the walk.
Livestock: There could be cattle in one field on the Avenue as the walk approaches Stonehenge.
Stiles: None.
Nearest vets: Stonehenge Vets, Larkhill Road, Durrington SP4 8DP.
☎ 01980 654404

Terrain

An undulating landscape with just one gentle climb along the Avenue towards Stonehenge. The walk follows a mixture of enclosed tracks and fieldpaths.

Where to park

The Woodhenge car park between Amesbury and Durrington (GR: 151433).
Map: OS Explorer 130 Salisbury & Stonehenge.

How to get there

Leave the A303 at Amesbury and follow the A345 northwards towards Upavon and Devizes. In just under 1 mile, turn left into the Woodhenge parking area.

Refreshments

Dogs are allowed at the Stonehenge Inn just along the A345 on the edge of Durrington. The pub is actually located within the ancient monument known as Durrington Walls, the largest prehistoric monument in the country. There is a daily carvery, with food available from 12 noon until 9:30 pm each day, apart from Sundays when food service ends at 9 pm. Breakfasts are also served each day, from 7 am in the week and from 8 am at weekends. ☎ 01722 790236. **Postcode**: SP4 8PN

The Walk

1 Pass through the bollards by the parking area before turning left to a gate and the **NT Durrington Walls** property. Walk ahead to the far left corner of this property, pass through a gateway and cross a road to a gate opposite. Walk across the field ahead, with a fence on the right, then down to a gate in

the bottom right corner of the field. Bear left and drop down to a track, the course of an old army railway line, and follow this track to the left. After 600 yards, and 100 yards before an electricity pylon, pass through a gap on the right to join a track. Follow this track – signposted to the **'Old King Barrows'** – for ¾ mile, before keeping on the track as it bears right.

2 After 50 yards, turn left at a junction with another **'King Barrows'** sign. Follow this track, it bears left along the way, to reach an information board about **'The Avenue'** and a handgate on the right in 350 yards. Pass through this gateway and walk across the field ahead, dropping downhill to reach a handgate in a fence in 600 yards. Beyond this gate, walk ahead to another information board before bearing left to walk uphill towards **Stonehenge**. On reaching a fence in front of this monument, turn right and follow the line of fences along to a gate and track in 300 yards. Follow this track to the right for 600 yards to a **'Cursus'** information board and gate on the right.

3 Continue along the track to the next handgate on the right and, beyond this handgate, walk across to the far left corner of the field ahead – this is now the course of the **Cursus**. Pass through a gate, cross a small paddock to another

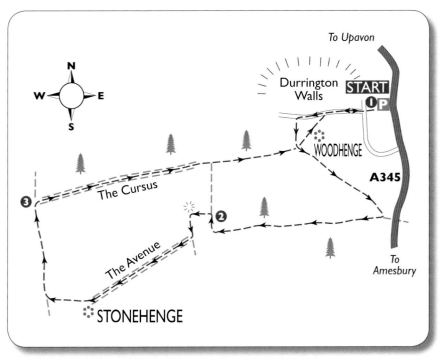

Stunning autumn colours at King Barrows.

gate and follow the left edge of the next field for ½ mile to a gate and track that leads to a crossroads. Follow the enclosed path opposite for ½ mile to a gap on the left by an **MoD sign**. Turn left up to a handgate and enter an enclosure that was passed earlier in the walk. Walk diagonally across the middle of this field to a gate and the road by the **Woodhenge monument**, before turning right, back to the parking area.

The Stourhead Estate

Dog walkers can enjoy late afternoon walks in the landscaped gardens at Stourhead.

There is a lot more to Stourhead than meets the eye. Most visitors walk down from the car park to the magical gardens, with the lake as its grand centrepiece, before visiting the Palladian mansion ... and that is it! This walk explores both of these admittedly fine attractions, as well as visiting so much more of the entire Stourhead Estate. Along the way the route initially passes ancient millponds, before climbing through woodland to reach King Alfred's Tower. This huge folly, allegedly built on a site where King Alfred once rallied his troops, commands magnificent views across Somerset, Dorset and Wiltshire. Below the folly lies Six Wells Bottom and St Peter's

Dog factors

· ·

Distance: 5 miles (excluding the detour to Alfred's Tower).
Road walking: There is a short section of road walking in Stourhead, with the remainder of the walk being traffic-free.
Livestock: There are occasionally sheep and cattle in one or two of the fields on the Stourhead Estate.
Stiles: None.
Nearest vets: Southill Vets, Manor Road, Mere BA12 6HY.
☎ 01963 33226

Pump, the source of the River Stour from which Stourhead takes its name. At the far end of this beautiful valley, having passed a series of fishponds, the walk climbs to an obelisk before passing Stourhead House itself. The clock arch and a walled garden bring the walk to a grand finale before a decision has to be taken – back up to the car park for the NT restaurant, or back down into the village for the delights of the Spread Eagle Inn. If your preference is Cowper's cup which 'cheers but doth not inebriate', then it is a left turn to the car park; otherwise a right turn! Dogs are welcome in the gardens at Stourhead from March to November after 4 pm on short fixed leads, and all day between December and February.

Terrain
Fieldpaths and woodland tracks, with one relatively gentle climb up to King Alfred's Tower.

Where to park
The National Trust car park at Stourhead (GR: 779340). **Map**: OS Explorer 142 Shepton Mallet & Mendip Hills East.

How to get there
Follow the A361 Frome bypass to its junction with the B3092 south of Frome. Follow the B3092 for 8 miles before taking the right turn signposted to Stourhead. In 200 yards, turn left into the National Trust's car park.

Refreshments
Whilst the Spread Eagle Inn at Stourhead does not welcome dogs inside, outside is a large courtyard area with tables and chairs where dogs are allowed. The pub is open all day every day, with food always available. ☎ 01747 840587. **Postcode**: BA12 6QE

The Walk

1 Walk through the reception area at the far side of the car park and follow a zigzag path downhill to the **Spread Eagle Inn**. Bear right out of the car park, turn left along the road and continue past **Stourhead Gardens** and on for 150 yards to an archway. Immediately past this archway, turn right and follow a track past a pond and onto a gate and cattle grid. Continue following the track ahead across an open field and past **Beech Cottage** on the right, to reach a gate and stile. Continue along the track to a fork, pass through the gateway ahead and continue following the right-of-way across a field to a gate and coniferous woodland.

2 Follow the path uphill for ¾ mile to a junction on the hilltop with a wide grassy ride. Detour to the left for 600 yards to explore **King Alfred's Tower** – but for the main walk, turn right and follow a grassy ride along to a gate. Continue following this grassy path across the left edge of the hilltop until a monument known as **St Peter's Pump**, the source of the **Stour**, comes into view in a valley on the right known as **Six Wells Bottom**. Turn right, drop

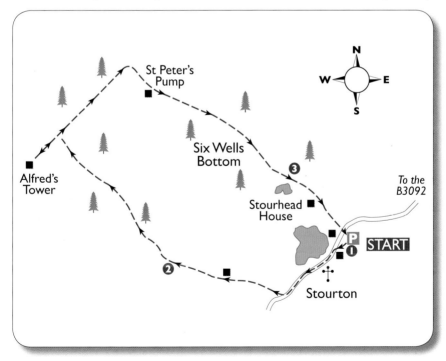

downhill to the monument and walk down through the valley for ¾ mile to reach some fishing ponds on the right.

3 At this point, bear left up to a gate in the top corner of the field, continue ahead along a track to the next gate and then climb a bank up to an **obelisk**. With your back to the obelisk inscription, bear half-left, walking across open parkland to reach a gravelled track in 100 yards. Follow this track to the right to the front of **Stourhead House**. Keep on the drive as it bears left away from the house and continue down to **Clock Arch**. Immediately before the arch, veer right onto a path that leads into the walled garden. By a pond on the right, turn left onto a path that crosses a bridge before rejoining the zigzag path followed at the outset. Follow this path back up to the car park.

Exploring the picturesque Stourton village.

Great Wishford and Grovely Wood

This is a walk you will keep coming back to.

This is a relaxing walk from the attractive village of Great Wishford, that lies in the Wylye Valley between Warminster and Salisbury, up onto the wooded hills to the south-west and deep into the ancient forest of Grovely Wood. Come this way on 29th May, Oak Apple Day, and you will find the locals enacting an ancient custom known as the Grovely Forest Rights. This annual ceremony is where the residents of Great Wishford claim their right to collect 'all kinde of deade snapping woode, boughs and stickes' from the local forest. Very early in the morning, the cry of 'Grovely, Grovely, Grovely and All Grovely' sounds forth, and the villagers proceed to the wood where an oak bough is cut. This bough is then decked in ribbons and carried ceremonially to Great Wishford church where it is hung from the tower. Whilst all of this fine detail will be lost on our four-footed friends, dogs will certainly enjoy the smells and sounds of the woodland where they can run off-lead for a canine adventure.

Terrain

A mixture of virtually traffic-free forestry access roads, woodland paths and enclosed tracks. There is a gentle climb from Great Wishford up into Grovely Wood.

Walking is thirsty work!

Dog factors

Distance: 5 miles.
Road walking: There is a very short section of road walking in Great Wishford at the start and finish of the walk. Once away from the village, the walk follows access roads and tracks to Grovely Wood, that can be used by the occasional vehicle.
Livestock: There are no issues with livestock on this walk.
Stiles: None.
Nearest vets: Avon Lodge Veterinary Group, 34 West Street, Wilton, SP2 0DG. ☎ 01722 742332

Where to park
On the roadside between Great Wishford church and the Royal Oak (GR: 079355). **Map**: OS Explorer 130 Salisbury & Stonehenge.

How to get there
Leave the A36 at Stoford, 3 miles north of Wilton, and follow an unclassified road signposted to Great Wishford. On entering the village, drive past the church and village school and park near the Royal Oak.

Refreshments
The Royal Oak in Great Wishford is a dog-friendly pub that also has a small garden area where dogs and their owners can relax in the fresh air. Food is served between 12 noon and 2 pm and 6 pm and 9 pm. ☎ 01722 790184
Postcode: SP2 0PD

The Walk

❶ Walk under the railway bridge by the **Royal Oak** and follow a quiet lane for just over 1 mile to the entrance to **Grovely Wood**. Where the road ends at the entrance to the woodland, follow a track uphill. After ¾ mile, carry straight on at a crossroads. In another 350 yards, shortly before a junction on the edge of the woodland, follow a footpath on the left – there is a waymark on a telegraph pole on the right.

❷ After ¼ mile, join a broad track and follow this past a barrier for ¾ mile to a crossroads, with a bridleway sign on a tree on the right. Turn left and

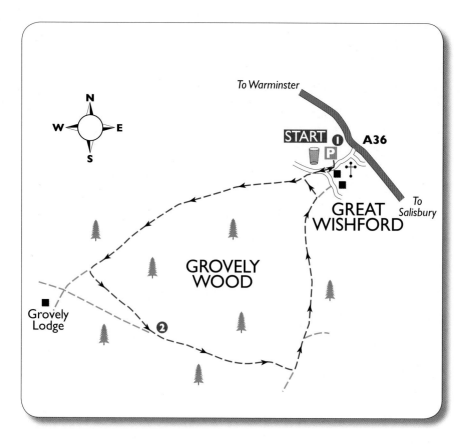

follow this bridleway, ignoring a grassy path that veers off on the right after 300 yards. Stay on this bridleway, it emerges from the woodland onto open downland, for just over 1 mile to a barrier on the edge of **Great Wishford**. Beyond this barrier, follow a track on the left to its junction with the road from the start of the walk. Turn right, pass under the railway bridge and return to the **Royal Oak**.

Coombe Bissett

There's plenty for a dog to explore at Grim's Ditch.

Coombe Bissett lies deep in the Ebble Valley, just a few miles west of Salisbury. All around lies archetypal Wiltshire downland that will, later in the day, provide fine walking country for both dogs and their owners. Early on in the walk, for example, there is Coombe Bissett Down, a nature reserve where the unimproved chalk grassland is home to a rich array of flora and butterflies during the summer months, including Adonis Blue and Chalkhill Blue, Dingy Skipper and Marbled White. Beyond the open

Dog factors

Distance: 5 miles.
Road walking: There are short sections of road walking in Coombe Bissett, and two roads have to be crossed along the way.
Livestock: Sheep often graze on Coombe Bissett Down, so be aware and keep your dog on a lead if necessary.
Stiles: There are stiles on Coombe Bissett Down but these have 'dog gates' on them. If you have a larger dog, there is a parallel lane that avoids this section of the walk.
Nearest vets: Endell Veterinary Group, 49 Endless Street, Salisbury SP1 3UH. ☎ 01722 333291

downland, the walk follows a series of tracks and byways, one of which borders a feature known as Grim's Ditch. These mysterious ditches appear in several locations across the south of England and are thought to be boundaries that demarcate ownership of land. Heading back into Coombe Bissett, along what the map shows as 'Old Blandford Road (Track)', look out for an isolated spire that penetrates the skyline; this is none other than Salisbury Cathedral with the surrounding city hidden away in a valley. This track is also a fine spot for foraging, in season the hedgerows are awash with blackberries and elder, sloes and rose hips.

Terrain

Following a gentle ascent out of Coombe Bissett, this is a walk across flat countryside until a descent at journey's end. The walk is mainly on fieldpaths and tracks, with one farm access road along the way.

Where to park

Park on Homington Road in Coombe Bissett, near the village shop (GR: 109264). **Map**: OS Explorer 130 Salisbury & Stonehenge.

How to get there

Coombe Bissett lies on the A354, four miles south-west of Salisbury's city centre. In the village, leave the main road by the church to follow Homington Road, signposted to the village shop.

Refreshments

Well-behaved dogs are guaranteed to be spoilt at the Fox & Goose in Coombe Bissett. The pub is open all day every day of the week, opening at 11 am Monday to Saturday and 12 noon on Sundays. ☎ 01722 718437

The Walk

. . . .

1 Walk away from the **A354** before taking the first right into **Shutts Lane**, leading to the school and village hall. After 150 yards, where the road bears right to the village hall, keep ahead on a bridleway. Ignoring one right turn along the way, follow this bridleway for 350 yards until it reaches a quiet lane. Just before this lane, turn right into a small car park, pass through a handgate and enter **Coombe Bissett Down**, a nature reserve. Follow the left edge of 5 fields to a stile on the left after 1 mile, just before some farm

A popular spot with local dog walkers.

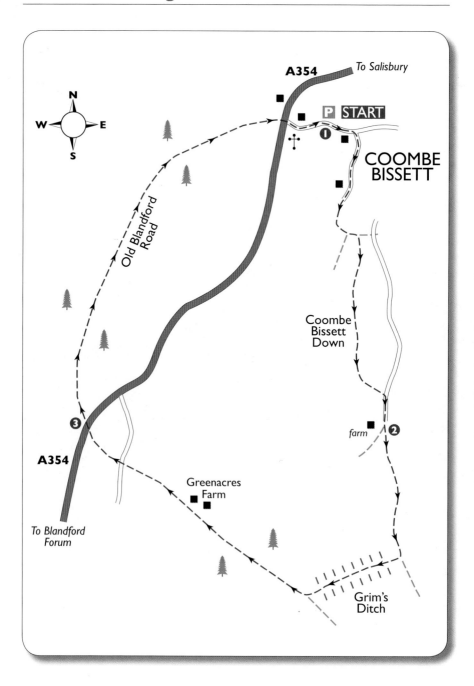

buildings. (If you have a larger dog, it might be easier to follow the lane to the east to reach these buildings, rather than negotiate a stile although there is a 'dog gate' on the stile.)

2 At a fork just past these farm buildings, keep left to follow a grassy path. In just over ½ mile, turn right along a track that borders **Grim's Ditch**. In ¼ mile, at a junction, follow a track – it becomes a metalled lane – for ¾ mile to its junction with a road. Cross over and follow the track opposite for ¼ mile through to the busy **A354**.

3 Follow the byway opposite for 2 miles to the **A354** in **Coombe Bissett**, by a green and the village church. This byway is the **Old Blandford Road** and is a well-defined track that poses no navigational issues. Turn left on reaching the main road in **Coombe Bissett** and then first right into **Homington Road** to return to the village shop.

Broad Chalke

The patio garden at the Queen's Head in Broad Chalke is perfect for thirsty dog walkers.

Broad Chalke lies just a few short miles west of Salisbury, deep in the heart of the Ebble Valley. The Ebble is one of five rivers that converge on the city, in this case the river having its confluence with the Avon in the water meadows to the south of the cathedral. Arguably the main attraction in the village is the Chalke Valley Stores, a shop, Post Office and coffee shop. This handsome building with walls of knapped flints was originally a Congregational Chapel, later becoming the local United Reformed Church. It became the village shop in 2013 and, the following year, was voted 'The Best Village Shop and Post Office in the UK' by the *Daily Telegraph* and the Countryside Alliance. All around the village lies archetypal chalk downland, with expansive views and big skies at every turn, that forms the central focus of this walk. There is also a section of the Old Shaftesbury Drove, a medieval track that ran from Shaftesbury to Salisbury which was used for moving livestock on foot between these two market towns. This is a walk that dogs will really enjoy because, once away from the village, the whole route is almost traffic-free, except the occasional farm vehicle.

Terrain
This walk follows enclosed paths and tracks across largely open downland. There is a gentle climb from Broad Chalke up onto Stoke Down, but nothing that is overly strenuous.

Where to park
Park on the roadside near the Chalke Valley Stores in Broad Chalke (GR: 039256). **Map**: OS Explorer 130 Salisbury & Stonehenge.

How to get there
Leave the A30 just west of Fovant, a village between Shaftesbury and Wilton, and follow the well-signposted road into Broad Chalke where Chalke Valley Stores lies in the centre of the village.

Refreshments
The Queen's Head in Broad Chalke welcomes everybody from locals and tourists to dog walkers and cyclists. Dating from the 18th century, you will enjoy 'traditional pub classics served with passion and flair'. The pub is open from 11 am until 11 pm every day, with food served between 12 noon and 9:30 pm, except on Sundays when food service finishes at 9 pm. ☎ 01722 780344.

Dog factors

Distance: 6½ miles.
Road walking: Very short sections of road walking in Broad Chalke at the start and finish of the walk.
Livestock: None, but keep an eye open for the occasional pheasant.
Stiles: None.
Nearest vets: The Pet Practice, Lower Road, Salisbury SP2 7PN.
☎ 01722 414000

The Walk

- -

1 With your back to the village store, follow the road to the right past the pub and around a right-hand bend before taking the first right in 100 yards, a cul de sac signposted to the **Queen's Head** car park. Follow this lane to where it ends by a thatched cottage, before continuing along the path that runs to the left of this property. After 120 yards, where the path emerges into the corner of an open field, walk ahead a few paces and continue following the path as it continues its course between hedgerows at the top of arable fields. In ½ mile, where the path reaches the corner of a field and a belt of trees, turn right into the adjoining field and follow a path down to a concrete farm road.

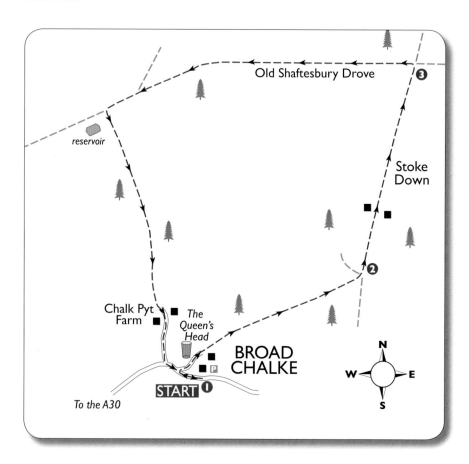

A winding road gently leads you back home.

2 Turn left and follow this road for 600 yards to a collection of farm buildings. Continue for ½ mile before veering right onto a grassy path running alongside the field boundary on the right – do not follow the track that runs inside the field itself and parallel to this path. After 350 yards, keep on the path as it bears right, away from the field to pass through some woodland before emerging into an arable field after 50 yards. Walk diagonally across the middle of this field, a few isolated trees marking the course of what is a bridleway. On the far side of the field, keep walking in the same direction through some woodland, ignoring side turns, until the bridleway joins a farm road after 250 yards. Follow this road up to a junction where it meets a track known as the **Old Shaftesbury Drove**.

3 Turn left and follow this drove for just under 2 miles to a left turn, immediately beyond which is a **reservoir** hidden in the trees. Turn left and follow a track for 1½ miles down to **Chalk Pyt Farm**. Continue past the farm buildings down to the road in **Broad Chalke**, walk ahead to pass the cul de sac on the left passed at the outset, and keep on the road as it bears left to bring you back to the village shop.

Tollard Royal and Cranborne Chase

Approaching Win Green.

Cranborne Chase is a vast chalk plateau that straddles the boundaries of Wiltshire, Dorset and Hampshire. The word 'Chase' is indicative of the area's former role as a royal hunting ground, in this case the sport was enjoyed by King John, Henry VIII and James I. It is an area of contrasts with the open chalk downland overlooking wooded valleys – or 'bottoms' as they are called in this neck of the woods. This walk heads out from Tollard Royal, home of King John's Hunting House, through Ashcombe Bottom and onto Win Hill. If the setting seems familiar, Ashcombe House and the surrounding land were formerly the home of Madonna and Guy Ritchie and made headlines in relation to access rights. Win Hill is also the highest point on the Chase, with commanding views that include the Isle of Wight and the Mendip Hills, the Quantock Hills and Milk Hill above the Vale of Pewsey. The hilltop is also classed as a 'Marilyn' – hills with a prominence of 150 metres – with the name coined as a punning contrast to the Scottish Munros. The return to Tollard Royal is by way of an enclosed track running across Berwick Down, where dogs can enjoy complete freedom to run off-lead.

Dog factors

Distance: 6 miles.
Road walking: None.
Livestock: There are occasionally sheep in Ashcombe Bottom where the main 'hazard' will be pheasants. If your dog is a hunter, then a lead is a must on this section of the walk.
Stiles: One stile to access Win Green.
Nearest vets: Longmead Veterinary Practice, Longmead, Shaftesbury, Dorset SP7 8PL. ☎ 01747 852064

Terrain
Well-defined footpaths and tracks, with open downland on Win Green. There is one very steep ascent onto Win Green itself, but the rewards are immense in terms of one of the best viewpoints in southern England.

Where to park
There is parking alongside a small pond at the southern end of Tollard Royal (GR: 945178). **Map**: OS Explorer 118 Shaftesbury & Cranborne Chase.

How to get there
Leave the A30 on the eastern side of Shaftesbury and follow the B3081 for six miles to Tollard Royal. The drive includes the infamous 'Zig-Zag Hill' that climbs onto the downland. Drive through the village until you see a small pond on the left.

Refreshments
The King John Inn at Tollard Royal welcomes clean dogs on leads. There is also a pleasant outside seated area that includes a raised garden. Fine food using the best local produce is served each day between 12 noon and 2:30 pm and 7 pm and 9:30 pm. ☎ 01725 516207. The open ground of Win Green is also an excellent spot for a picnic halfway around the walk.

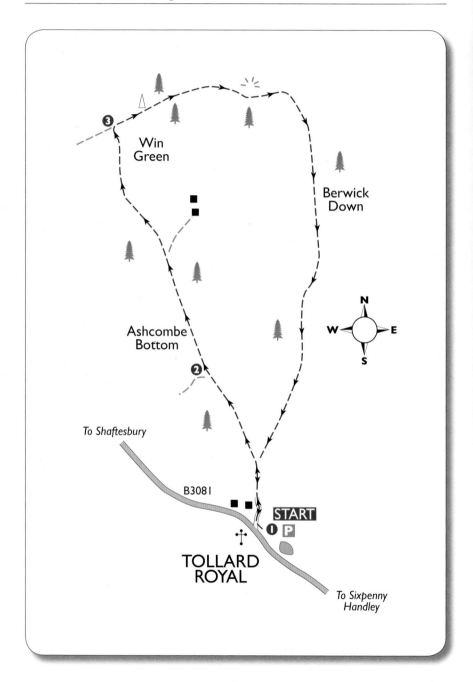

All stiles carefully checked by Finn!

The Walk

❶ Facing the pond from the parking area, follow a side lane on the left away from the **B3081**. After 100 yards, at a fork, veer left off the main route along a grassy track. Beyond a gate, follow a path – the **Wessex Ridgeway** – through a valley, with a steep hillside on the right. In ¾ mile, pass through a handgate and cross the corner of an enclosure to another handgate.

❷ Turn right and continue following the path through the valley, shown as **Ashcombe Bottom** on the OS map. After ½ mile, beyond a gate, continue along a chalk and flint path. Continue following the path, with clear signs at two junctions pointing out that the right turns are private, for ¾ mile to a junction at the top of a short steep climb. Turn left and follow a path steeply uphill through some woodland to a handgate. Continue uphill across some open grassland, with a fence on the left, to a stile in the top left corner of the **National Trust's Win Green** property.

3 Cross this stile and turn right to walk across to a trig point and topograph just before a hilltop copse. Continue across the hilltop, passing to the right of the copse, to pick up a grassy path that drops downhill to a gate. Beyond this gate, follow a chalk track for 2¾ miles across **Berwick Down**, and all the way back to the duckpond and parking space in **Tollard Royal**.